# my first book of **pilates**

### Miranda Morgan

BARNES
&NOBLE
BOOKS
NEW YORK

This edition published by Barnes & Noble, Inc.,
by arrangement with Elwin Street Limited

Copyright © Elwin Street Limited, 2003

2003 Barnes & Noble Books

M 10 9 8 7 6 5 4 3 2 1

ISBN 0-7607-4042-9

Conceived and produced by Elwin Street Limited
35 Charlotte Road
London EC2A 3PD
www.elwinstreet.com

Design: Adelle Morris
Photography: Mike Prior
Model: Caroline Cooper

Printed in Singapore

# contents

# what is **pilates?**

# what is **pilates?**

Once the exclusive secret of dancers, actors, and celebrities, Pilates is now one of the fastest growing exercise programs in the world. The reason? First, practically anyone can do it, and second, it works. That's because Pilates is a unique way of thinking about your body; a way of exercising your muscles and reshaping your body to feel stronger, longer, and leaner.

Like yoga and the Alexander technique, Pilates is an intelligent exercise that calls for you to engage your body and mind in a series of precise, focused exercises. Sometimes the exercises are so subtle that you wonder if they're doing anything at all, but Pilates is all about retraining your body and teaching it the good habits that will keep it strong and supple for the rest of your life.

Pilates is a total body-conditioning workout that builds core strength, develops a graceful posture, and creates a properly aligned body. It is low impact and non-competitive, which means you can create a strong balanced body without building biceps and breaking into a sweat. Instead of concentrating on superficial muscles it builds the deep muscles that protect the spine. Pilates also leaves you feeling more energetic and happy about yourself.

This book is a basic introduction to Pilates that outlines the key principles, cuts through the jargon, and shows you some of the positions to start you on your way. Hopefully, it will encourage you to develop an interest in Pilates and achieve the body you want.  But remember to be patient, take care, and have fun.

## History of pilates

The Pilates method is based on the work of one man: Joseph Pilates. Born in 1880 in Dusseldorf, Germany, Joseph Pilates was a sickly child. Undaunted, he studied anatomy and became a physical trainer, experimenting with yoga, gymnastics, skiing, self-defense techniques, dance, circuit training, and weight training. In his early thirties he moved to England, and when World War I broke out, Pilates, as a German national, was interred on the Isle of Man. It was here that he developed the therapeutic side of his fitness program, helping with the rehabilitation of patients in the camp. He later returned to Germany, but in 1926 he emigrated to the U.S.A.

Together with his wife, Clara, whom he met on the boat to New York, he set up the Pilates Studio in the same building as the New York City Ballet, establishing the strong link between Pilates and dance that has continued to this day (presently, about 80 percent of Pilates-based teachers have traditional dance backgrounds).

Pilates never set down a specific training program, so since his death in 1967 devotees have developed his early methods in a variety of different ways.

For years, Pilates remained the preserve of dancers, athletes, and actors, but in the 1990s, as the popularity of high impact fitness programs decreased, Pilates began to gain widespread recognition. It's now reckoned to be one of the fastest growing fitness programs in the world. Not bad for a sick kid from Dusseldorf.

# benefits of **pilates**

**Tones muscles** Pilates can tone your buttocks, thighs, arms, and shoulders, as well as give you a flatter stomach and a trimmer waist. It gives you stronger, leaner muscles without the stress of jogging or the gym, and it does all this without adding bulk, so you'll look more like a dancer than a body builder.

**Improves posture** You'll improve your posture with Pilates, which means you'll stand taller and straighter than before, therefore boosting your self-confidence.

**Low impact** Pilates complements aerobic exercise and is low impact, so there's less chance of you straining your body or injuring yourself.

**Repairs injuries** Pilates can help prevent injuries for dancers and athletes and can even heal injuries (especially those related to the back) when it is used as a therapy.

**Full body workout** Pilates also boosts the immune system, increases bone density, makes your joints more mobile, and your whole body more flexible.

**Stress buster** The focus on breathing will leave you feeling revitalized rather than exhausted, and after a hard day at the office it's a great stress buster. Pilates really does make you feel better.

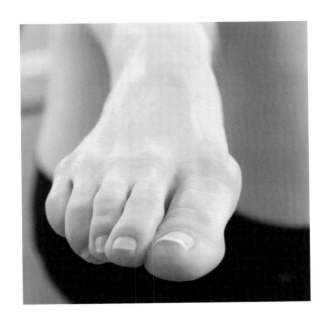

# basic **principles**

## breath

Breath is life; it's the first and last thing we do in this world, and it's closely linked to both balance and body control. Most of us take it for granted, but in Pilates you will need to learn a new breathing technique called "lateral" breathing. You will also usually find that an in-breath is a preparation for starting a movement, while an out-breath accompanies each movement. The most important thing is to keep breathing throughout; hold your breath and you might pass out.

## concentration

Go to most gyms and you'll find people zoning out on repetitive exercise machines, listening to music or even watching TV. Joseph Pilates would be horrified. Pilates is "the thinking way of moving," and you can't do any of the exercises properly without using your mind. This concentrated activity also has benefits in the rest of your life, giving you greater clarity and reducing stress.

## control

Try to stand on one foot. Within seconds, you'll most likely wobble and fall. But if you try this every day, then after a week you should be able to stand for a full minute. Control is about mastering your body and doing things you would otherwise find impossible. It's not for nothing that Joseph Pilates called his method "Contrology," so during Pilates it is important to keep all your movements slow and measured.

## centering

Anything that moves, lifts, or carries needs a strong center or base. In Pilates, this means centering two things. First, it means being able to remain steady and balanced with good posture whatever you are doing. Second, it means engaging the center of your body, the ring of core muscles that run around your body from just below your ribs to the tops of your legs.

## precision

Pilates is about quality, not quantity. Before breezing through the exercises, it's worth bearing in mind that Pilates calls for complete co-ordination. That means making sure that your body is well aligned, you are breathing correctly, you are well centered, and your movements are fluid. Such precision can be frustrating at first, but in Pilates, it is only through a repetition of small, precise movement patterns that you will see results.

## flow

It's no great surprise that an exercise program that is so closely connected to dance should highlight the importance of flowing movement. Each exercise has a pattern with identifiable stages that must be executed in a harmonious and continuous flow. In turn, the individual exercises can then be combined to flow one after the other. Done well, Pilates can be both strong and graceful.

you and **pilates**

# you and **pilates**

## What do you want?

Each person comes to Pilates with a different goal, whether that means wanting to touch their toes, correct their posture, or complement another sport. This goal will determine where and how you take your Pilates practice further. Think about why you are taking up Pilates and share it with your Pilates teacher.

### Are you simply curious?
Go along to a class and try it out.

### Are you looking for a fitness program?
Pilates provides a full workout, but it takes time. Be patient and you will begin to see the results within a matter of months.

### Do you want a better body?
Pilates can help you strengthen and lengthen your muscles, but if you want to lose weight you should do some cardiovascular training and follow a suitable nutritional program.

### Are you looking for help with an injury?
Always consult a physician before taking up a new form of exercise, and always tell your Pilates teacher if you have a specific health concern.

### Are you pregnant?
Congratulations! Pilates has numerous benefits to help you. Look for special prenatal classes in your area.

### Are you into sports?
Pilates can be a good supplement to sports, offsetting imbalances.

# What are you like?

It's important to be clear about what sort of person you are when embarking on a Pilates practice. After all, it's your body.

### How often are you prepared to practice?

You get out what you put in, so draw up a schedule of practice times; a minimum of ten minutes three times a week.

### What is there nearby?

Have a look around and see what classes there are in your area. You can also pick up information on the Internet and in gyms.

### What do you expect to achieve?

Patience pays dividends.

### Are you looking for a slower or more vigorous approach?

Pilates teaching depends on the teacher's approach and the level of the class. Always go to the level that is right for you.

### How much money are you prepared to spend?

A one-to-one will be tailored to your needs, but a gym will be cheaper and more sociable.

### Where are you going to practice?

Try and find somewhere quiet.

Remember, you're the one who's going to be breathing, moving, and thinking out there on the mat. Pilates is individual and non-competitive, so take responsibility for your own practice and you'll enjoy it a hundred times more.

# pilates **styles**

Joseph Pilates never set down a specific training program, and in 2000 a court ruled that the name "Pilates" could not be trademarked, so it now acts as a generic word like yoga. What all that means is that the Pilates scene is very mixed, with "Pilates" and "Pilates-based" courses being taught by thousands of people. Bearing in mind Pilates is also a big business, you should be clear about what you're looking for and what you expect.

Pilates teachers come from many different backgrounds, so some will emphasize a rapidly moving, high-energy pace, and others will suggest a slower, more concentrated approach. In this book we have tried to explain the foundation exercises of the two approaches. The basic truth is that no two Pilates teachers are the same, whether they come from New York or the North Pole. Whether you are going to a gym or a studio, talk with your teacher before you start, asking them what sort of training they have had and what approach they take.

# fitness and **rehabilitation**

Pilates can be divided into two broad groups: fitness and rehabilitation.

## fitness pilates

There are three main groups of people who look to Pilates for fitness.

Some people simply want to "get fit" and increase their general strength, stamina, and flexibility.

Others want a more performance-related approach, treating Pilates as sports training.

A third group want to improve their posture and alignment through remedial therapy.

Instruction can now be found through matwork classes, equipment classes, studio sessions, books, and videos.

Teachers will include dancers, gym instructors, Alexander teachers, yoga and aerobics teachers, and ex-clients of the Pilates Method.

## rehabilitation pilates

More and more people are now going to Pilates after a whole range of injuries, including back problems, joint injuries, and neck trauma. This usually means being taught one-to-one and will probably involve work on a range of specially designed Pilates equipment.

Teachers might include physiotherapists, osteopaths, chiropractors or remedial therapists.

## matwork

Matwork requires very little equipment and can be done at home or at the gym, so it is the most accessible and widespread way to learn Pilates. A matwork class involves between four and 25 people at a gym or a studio following the same exercise routine set by a teacher. Levels are usually split into beginner, intermediate, and advanced, but the routine for each group will differ from teacher to teacher. Matwork fits into a pattern of exercise that most people are familiar with. However, Pilates is by its nature a very individual approach, and it's sometimes difficult to address special needs. If you have the money then a couple of private lessons with a good teacher can set you up for life.

## pilates studio

Done properly, a Pilates studio has an atmosphere all of its own, unlike any gym or health club. Think of it as a pure Pilates paradise. There will usually be limited numbers in each session so you will receive more individual attention, with closer correction and more specialized exercises. This is especially good if you have a particular condition for which you need help. You are also likely to encounter some of the equipment involved in classic Pilates such as the Reformer, Cadillac, Wunda Chair, and Magic Circle. However, each studio will have a different approach and varying resources. It will also be more expensive and you will have to make specific appointments.

## one-to-one

Because Pilates is all about you, the more individualized the attention, the greater the insight into your own particular needs. Needless to say, you pay for the privilege, with private classes the most expensive, but they can provide a foundation that is invaluable.

**One-to-One studio sessions:** Many studios will recommend a few one-to-one sessions to work out your particular needs and start your Pilates tuition on a firm foundation. The sessions might be slightly shorter and may involve matwork or Pilates equipment.

**Private lessons:** There are many private Pilates teachers who will make home visits, but check their approach and their credentials first. Convenient and concentrated, private tuition will give you a very good grounding, but remember that it's your body; you're the one who has to take responsibility for your own program.

## books, videos, tapes

The cheapest method of all is to teach yourself. There are many books and videos on the market now and the collective experience they contain is invaluable. That said, nothing beats learning Pilates face-to-face. A good teacher will be able to establish a correct routine and a regular class will give you a solid basis to motivate you in your practice.

# equipment

Joseph Pilates developed a series of machines to use as part of his exercise program that you may encounter at a specialist Pilates studio.

They look weird (tables with seats and pullies, boxes, and sliding parts) and they sound weird (the Reformer, the Cadillac, the Wunda Chair, and the Magic Circle), but they're really just another way of working on the body and developing the exercises.

Strangely enough, unlike traditional weights, where more is added as you get stronger, Pilates exercise tension is often reduced as students gain strength. This is because they work on resistance ratio rather than load. As control of the body's center improves it becomes more important to challenge balance and coordination. This in turn lengthens and tones muscles and enhances the body's flexibility.

## the reformer

Otherwise known as the "Rack", because of its resemblance to an instrument of torture, the Reformer is a bedlike platform that slides back and forth on tracks.

It is the piece of equipment with which Joseph Pilates started most of his clients and is still the most popular Pilates equipment today. It provides support while you work on different parts of the body and allows you to do a range of different exercises.

## the cadillac

Another bedlike contraption with springs attached to the sides, the Cadillac, otherwise known as the "Four-poster," provides ballet-based flexibility and stability.

## the wunda chair

You can do more than 41 different exercises, plus variations, on the Wunda Chair, most of them building on abdominal strength. It is a backless box containing more fiendish springs. Special moves include the Washer Woman, the Pike, and the Jacknife.

## the magic circle

This is a circle with pads to support your hands or ankles which provides a low level of resistance as you push against it. It is not key studio equipment but is instead portable and can strengthen and develop even the hard-to-reach areas like your pelvic floor muscles.

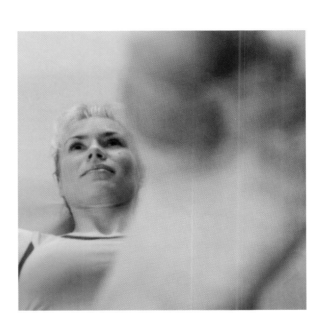

body **awareness**

# body **awareness**

Most of us are not very kind to our bodies. We slump over desks, walk around in high heels, drive rather than walk, and slouch around on sofas in the evening. This kind of living plays havoc with our posture, leaving us with all sorts of aches and pains. Sooner or later many of us end up with our bodies out of shape, our heads bowed and our spines bent.

You can spot someone with a Pilates body from a mile off; lean and straight, their shoulders back and their whole body engaged. That's because Pilates teaches you the secret of body symmetry, aligning your body so that you not only look good but feel much more comfortable as well. The correct alignment of the body is the basis for easy, comfortable movement throughout your life.

## the pilates posture

People with good posture look better. Good posture makes you feel better, too. Poor posture can contribute to ailments, and adopting a correct posture allows your internal organs to work optimally.

Look at yourself in a full-length mirror. Are your shoulders level? Is there an equal distance between your ears and your shoulders? Are your hips and kneecaps aligned? If you stand sideways, your head should be centered over your body, your neck long, and your spine should be erect but relaxed.

If this isn't you then don't despair. Pilates might be able to help.

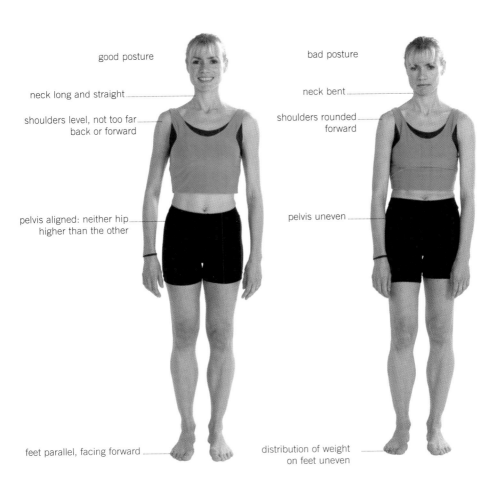

good posture

bad posture

neck long and straight

neck bent

shoulders level, not too far
back or forward

shoulders rounded
forward

pelvis aligned: neither hip
higher than the other

pelvis uneven

feet parallel, facing forward

distribution of weight
on feet uneven

## the spine

The spine is the body's central axis, made up from 34 individual bones or vertebrae that interlock and are bound together by ligaments. Each pair is cushioned by a cartilage layer and separated by a cartilage disk, which allows a small degree of movement. From behind the spine will appear straight, but from the side you will see that it has four natural curves: the cervical curve (neck), thoracic curve (upper back), lumbar curve (lower back), and sacral curve (tailbox). These act as a shock absorber and should be properly aligned during any Pilates exercise. Each time you start a routine, you should make sure that you realign your posture, whether you are standing or lying down. The best way to do that is to relax, so that the spine falls into its natural, neutral position.

Each vertebra is connected to the next by ligaments that control its range of movement. A cartilage disk between each vertebra prevents friction. In Pilates you should try to consciously engage each vertebra, one by one. Joseph Pilates said it was like "using the spine like a wheel" and these days it's called "spinal articulation". This increases the spine's flexibility and reduces the risk of injury.

## neutral pelvis

The pelvis is the base of support for your body. The position of your pelvis can effect your spinal alignment and posture. Viewed from the side, the pelvis should be held in a way that maintains the normal concave curve of the lower back of the spine: the lumbar curve. If the pelvis tips forward or back then this can create back strain.

In Pilates you should aim to achieve a "neutral pelvis," which really means defining the place where your spine rests while preserving all of its natural curves. While reasonably easy to do when standing up, such alignment is more difficult when lying down.

Do not arch your back

Avoid flattening your back

Correctly aligned, neither flattened nor arched

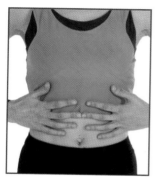

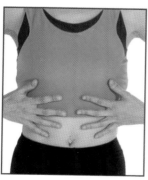

## lateral breathing

Efficient breathing is essential in any physical exercise and Pilates advocated filling the lungs entirely and emptying the lungs completely. Pilates practices "lateral" breathing, which expands the ribs sideways with each breath. Basically, it means breathing into the whole of the chest rather than the stomach. This allows us to keep the abdominal muscles engaged throughout breathing, which will greatly improve the strength of your "center." Practice the following exercise to demonstrate the way your ribs expand and contract.

1. Place your hands, fingertips touching, on your ribs.
2. Breathe in and watch your hands move apart.
3. Breathe out and watch your hands move together.

In most Pilates movements you will inhale before initiating a movement. As you begin to exhale you may then start the movement.

# the shoulders

Sometimes it can seem like we carry the world on our shoulders. Sadly, it sometimes looks that way as well. The shoulders and the neck store tension, seizing up when we're stressed. Don't hunch your shoulders or let them slope forward and make sure your shoulder blades slide down your back. This will lengthen the neck, strengthen the back and eliminate neck and shoulder tension.

Shoulder blades are two free-floating triangles that migrate downward and inward toward the spine. Continue to open the chest as you press the wings down and back. When lying down, imagine your shoulder blades pinned to the mat.

## core muscles

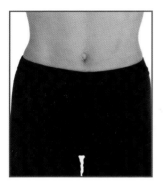

Like a tree, the branches are only as good as the trunk is strong, and in a human body this trunk is made up of a ring of muscles that run around the lower abdomen. These are the abdominal muscles, buttock muscles, and lower back muscles that support the spine and pelvis and form the center of strength and control for the rest of your body. In Pilates they are sometimes called the the "core muscles," the "powerhouse" or the "girdle of strength."

**You have three types of abdominal muscles.** The "six-pack," or rectus abdominus, is the one that gets all the press, but you must make sure it doesn't become over dominant. Underneath the "six-pack" are the external and internal obliques, muscles that wrap themselves around the waist and which are active in twisting and turning movements. Underneath all the others is the inner core or transverse abdominals. When contracted, they pull the abdominal wall toward the spine, decreasing the dimension of your waist. Pilates trains you to engage your core muscles as you begin every movement.

# zipping up

Abdominal muscles run lengthwise, diagonally, and horizontally. It is these latter muscles, called the transverse abdominals, that Pilates looks to develop and that encircle the waistline from front to back. When contracted they pull the abdominal wall toward the spine, decreasing the dimension of your waist. This action involves drawing up and in the muscles of the pelvic floor and hollowing the lower abdomen back toward the spine. When you do it, think of zipping up and hollowing your stomach, drawing back the abdominals toward the spine and sucking in. It is very difficult to keep the center strong while you breathe in and out and it is very important that you do not shorten the waist, round the shoulders forward, or thrust the hips under just to pull your waistline in.

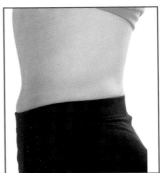

# the **exercises**

# before you **begin**

**Practice pilates on an empty stomach** That means four hours after a heavy meal or two hours after a snack. Drink water before the practice so you don't dehydrate.

**Wear comfortable clothes** Sometimes it is best to wear something tight-fitting like a leotard to make sure you can be aware of your body movement.

**Find some quiet** Practice in a quiet area on a folded mat or carpeted floor. The atmosphere should be relaxed, without music or conversation.

**Find a good teacher** A good teacher will be able to establish a correct routine and a regular class will give you a solid basis to motivate you in your practice.

**Pilates isn't a race** Pilates is non-competitive, so don't worry about the person next to you.

**Be realistic** Integrate Pilates into your life. That means being realistic about how much you are prepared to do. Start with ten minutes of exercise between one and six times a week.

**Breathe throughout** Remember to breathe throughout the exercises, practicing the lateral breathing that expands your ribcage sideways with each breath.

**Balance the exercises** Make sure you practice different exercises to create a balanced sequence. If you do an exercise that stretches one side of your body, then you always need to repeat the exercise on the other side.

**Take care** As with all exercise routines, you should seek medical advice first, especially if you already suffer from an illness or injury. Read the "Take Care" sections throughout the book and refrain from doing anything that causes pain. Don't practice exercises if you have a fever and remember to take things easy during menstruation.

**Follow the guide** Take note of the easy-to-use guide below. Make sure you follow the circles to practice the "basic" and "beginners" exercises first. Read the directions carefully, practicing the exercises in continuous, flowing movements. Above all, listen to your body. Pilates takes time, but the results are definitely worth it.

 basic        ●● beginners         intermediate

# Stand and center

Before any exercises, you should always make sure you are correctly centered.

**The exercise** 1. Stand with your feet hip width apart. Spread your toes, making sure the soles of your feet are making full contact with the floor. 2. From this central base, slowly sway in a circle, without moving your feet and maintaining your balance at all times. 4. Decrease the circles until you come back to center, your shoulders relaxed, your spine straight and your pelvis neutral.

**Take care** Maintain balance and comfort at all times. Relax.

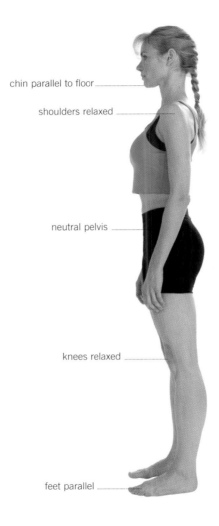

chin parallel to floor

shoulders relaxed

neutral pelvis

knees relaxed

feet parallel

# Dumb waiter

Opens the chest and strengthens
the muscles that turn the
shoulder joint outward.
Remember to let your shoulder
blades slide down your back.

**The exercise** 1. Breathe in.
2. Breathe out, zip up, and
hollow. 3. Keeping your
elbows to your sides, take
your hands backward.
Breathe in, opening the chest
and working the muscles
between the shoulder blades.
Keep the shoulder blades down.
4. Breathe out and return the
hands to the starting position.

**Take care** Do not allow the
upper back or stomach to arch
as you take the arms back. Keep
your neck released.

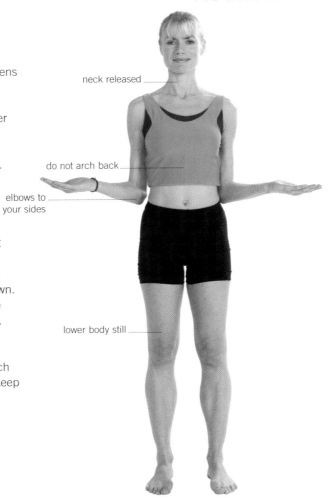

neck released

do not arch back

elbows to
your sides

lower body still

# Arm circle

Strengthens the shoulder girdle, taking the muscles through their full range sideways, above the head and back.

**The Exercise** 1. Open your arms from the shoulder joints so that your palms face the ceiling. Bend the elbows a little. 2. Breathe in, zip up, and hollow. 3. Breathe out slowly, drawing a big half-circle with your fingers from your thighs to high above your head. 4. Breathe in. 5. On a slow out-breath reverse the movement so that you draw a half-circle from above your head back down to your thighs. 6. Repeat three times, then shake your body and shoulders and walk around.

**Take care** Go gently at first; lack of use can stiffen the shoulder joint.

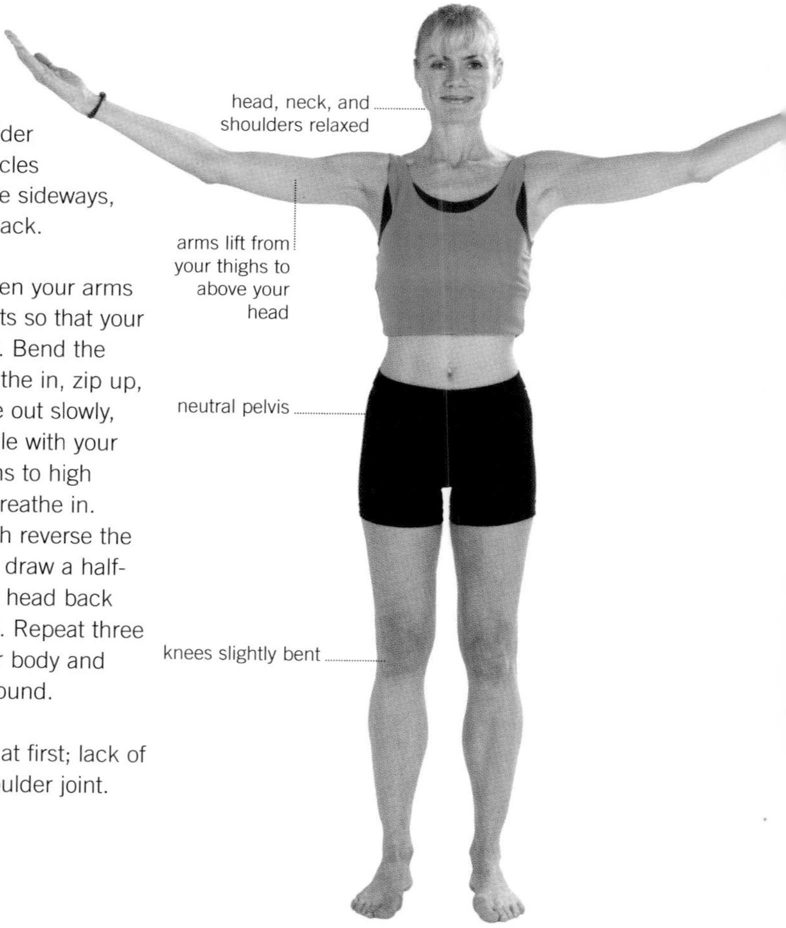

head, neck, and shoulders relaxed

arms lift from your thighs to above your head

neutral pelvis

knees slightly bent

# Side reaches

Stretches the sides, especially the waist muscles, and stabilizes the shoulder.

**The Exercise** 1. Stand with your feet hip width apart, your weight evenly balanced. Soften your knees. 2. Breathe in and reach your hand up to the side. 3. Breathe out, zip up, and hollow. Reach over. Make sure you go to the side and not forward or backward. 4. Breathe in and keep lengthening upward. 5. Breathe out, still zipped and hollowed, and slowly return to upright, then lower the arm. 6. Repeat five times to each side.

**Take care** Do not bend too far.

keep your head on top of your spine, looking forward

keep lengthening upward

neutral pelvis

other arm slides downward as you bend

# Roll downs

Develops use of the spine, using the core muscles to direct and control the mobility. A classic Pilates exercise: deceptively easy and very effective.

**The Exercise** 1. Stand with your feet hip width apart, your weight evenly balanced. 2. Find your neutral pelvis. 3. Breathe in, letting your shoulders slide down your back. 4. Breathe out slowly, zip up, and hollow. Drop your chin onto your chest and allow the weight of your head to make you roll forward slowly. Keep your knees and pelvis stable. 5. Breathe in as you let your head and arms hang. Don't collapse the back. 6. Breathe out as you drop your tailbone down and slowly come up to standing tall, rolling through the spine bone by bone. Your head uncurls last. Repeat five times.

**Take care** Go straight forward; do not sway to one side. Keep the weight evenly balanced and try not to lean forward or backward onto the heels.

let your head and neck relax

go down centrally

keep your knees and pelvis stable

do not roll the feet in or out

# Relaxation position

In all floor exercises it is vital to prepare your mind and body for exercise and be aware of body alignment.

**The Exercise**  1. Lie flat on your back. Bend your knees and place your feet on the floor hip width apart. Place your hands on your abdomen. 2. Feel your body relaxing into the floor, your muscles softening and your spine lengthening. Relax your jaw and facial muscles. 3. To find neutral pelvis, roll your pelvis slowly from one side ro another. 4. Next, roll your pelvis slowly back and forth until you return to neutral.

allow your whole body to widen and lengthen

release your neck

Keep your feet parallel, your toes in the same line

release your thighs and soften the area around your hips

# Head and neck rolls

Releases tension from the neck.

**The Exercise** 1. Lie in the relaxation position looking straight ahead. Focus on relaxing the neck muscles. 2. Roll your head slowly from side to side. Allow the weight of the head to govern the movement. 3. Lengthen the neck and gently tuck the chin in. 4. Release your neck. Keep the back of your neck lengthened. Allow your shoulder blades to sink into the floor. 5. Repeat rolling to the side and tucking your chin five times.

**Take care** Do not force it or rush it. Try to roll the head directly to the side, rotating it around its central axis.

allow your head to govern the weight of the movement

relax the neck muscles

roll your head gently to the side

# Backstroke

Encourages good movement in the body, reprogramming the muscles. Coordinates the opposite arm and leg.

**The Exercise** 1. Start in the relaxation position. Breathe in to prepare. 2. Breathe out, zip up, and hollow. Slide the left leg away along the floor and take the right arm above you in a backstroke movement. 3. Keep the pelvis neutral, stable, and still, and the core muscles engaged. 4. Breathe in, still zipped up and hollowed, and return the limbs to the starting position. Repeat five times on each side.

**Take care** These are the basic learning skills, invaluable in learning the more difficult exercises.

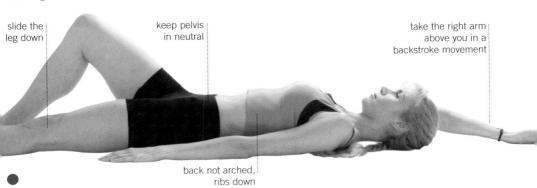

slide the leg down

keep pelvis in neutral

take the right arm above you in a backstroke movement

back not arched, ribs down

# Side rolls

Works the spine and waist muscles.

**The Exercise** 1. Start in the relaxation position. 2. Stretch your arms out to the side. Bend your knees and ankles together. 3. Breathe in. 4. Breathe out, zip up, and hollow. Roll your head in one direction and your knees in the other. Keep your knees closed and your opposite shoulder down on the floor. Only roll a little way to start with. 5. As you breathe out again, bring the knees back to the starting position and then the head. 6. Repeat eight times in each direction.

**Take Care** Keep the pelvis in neutral.

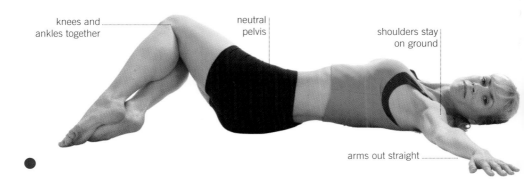

knees and ankles together

neutral pelvis

shoulders stay on ground

arms out straight

# Hamstring stretch

Stretches the hamstrings, the group of muscles in the back of the legs that flex and bend the knee. You will need a long scarf or strap to stretch against.

**The Exercise** 1. Start in relaxation position. 2. Wrap the scarf over the sole of your foot and hold the ends so that you can stretch the leg correctly. To stretch your hamstrings, your hips need to be square. 3. Breathe in to prepare. 4. Breathe out to zip up and hollow, and slowly lengthen your leg as if pulling your heel toward the ceiling. Keep your whole body relaxed. 5. Repeat on the other side.

**Take care** Stretch equally in each leg.

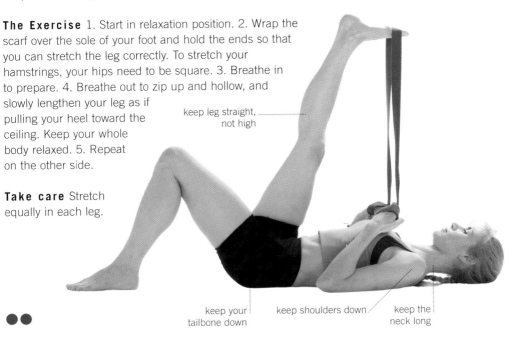

keep leg straight, not high

keep your tailbone down

keep shoulders down

keep the neck long

# Inner thigh squeeze

Works the pelvic floor and the core muscles as well as strengthening the inner thighs. Great for sciatica. Equipment: a ball or cushion to squeeze.

**The exercise** 1. Lie on your back in the neutral position with your feet together, flat on the floor. Place a cushion between your knees. 2. Breathe in. 3. Breathe out, zip up, and hollow. Squeeze the cushion between your knees using only your inner thigh muscles. Aim to hold for a count of ten, keeping the pelvis in neutral and the tailbone down on the floor, lengthening away. 4. Release. Repeat six times.

**Take care** Do not hold your breath. Keep your neck released and your jaw soft.

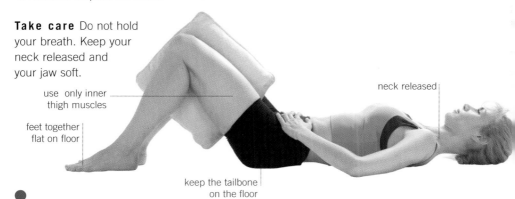

use only inner
thigh muscles

feet together
flat on floor

neck released

keep the tailbone
on the floor

# Spine curl

A core skill for the rest of your practice. It requires you to peel your spine off the mat vertebra by vertebra like a pearl necklace.

**The exercise** 1. Lie in the relaxation position. Release your neck and shoulders. 2. Breathe in. 3. As you breathe out, tilt your pelvis so that your lower back sinks into the mat and your pubic bone lifts toward the ceiling. 4. Breathe in. Breathe out to lower yourself back down. 5. Repeat, lifting a little more of the spine off the floor each time until you have lifted your whole abdomen up to your shoulder blades. Hold the position and take an in-breath. 6. As you breathe out, reverse the movement, replacing the spine bone by bone. Complete four full curls.

**Take care** Do not attempt if you have disk problems.

do not curl up too high

keep the pressure through your feet equal

"articulate the spine"

arms flat on floor

# Curl ups

Strengthens the abdominals. As with all exercises, zip up and hollow for the entire movement and coordinate with the breath.

**The Exercise** 1. Lie in relaxation position. Make sure pelvis is in neutral. 2. Breathe in. 3. As you breathe out, engage your core muscles and start to curl your chin in toward your head. Visualize the vertebra peeling off the mat. Make sure that your abdominals stay engaged, the pelvis square and stable. 4. On the next outbreath slowly curl back down. Repeat ten times.

**Take care** Do not bulge your stomach. Avoid if you have neck problems.

hands straight out or
supporting the neck

feet flat and
parallel on floor

try not to grip
around the hips

do not strain neck

# Release position

Another relaxation exercise, this allows your neck and spine
to lengthen and your abdominal muscles to relax.

**The Exercise** Take hold of your knees and pull them towards
your chest. Breathe easily and feel your spine lengthening.
Allow your abdominal muscles to relax.

**Take care** Do this exercise with caution if you have lower
back pain.

knees bent

keep tailbone
down

lengthen spine
and neck

shoulders
relaxed

# The dart 1

Strengthens the lower and upper back muscles and creates awareness of the shoulder blades.

**The Exercise** 1. Lie on your front with your forehead on the floor. Keep your arms down at your side, palms facing your body. 2. Breathe in and lengthen through the spine, tuck your chin in. 3. Draw up your abdominals. Breathe out and feel your shoulder blades slide down your back, lengthening your fingers away from you down toward your feet. The top of the head stays lengthening away from you. Keep looking straight down at the floor. 4. Return to your starting position on the in-breath. 5. Repeat six times.

**Take care** Do not expect to move very far during this exercise.

do not tip your head back or arch from neck

keep feet on floor

# The dart 2

Lengthens and strengthens the back muscles.

**The Exercise**  1. Start in the dart. 2. Breathe in and lengthen through the spine, tucking your chin in gently. 3. Breathe out, zip up, and hollow and feel the shoulder blades slide down your back, lengthening your fingers away from your center down toward your feet. The top of your head stays lengthening away from you. 4. Using the mid-back muscles, slowly raise the upper body from the floor. Keep looking straight down. Do not tip your head back. Breathe in and feel the length of the body. 5. Breathe out, still zipped and hollowed, and slowly lower.

**Take care**  Stop if you feel at all uncomfortable in lower back.

feet stay on floor

do not tip head back

keep hollowing the lower abdominals

# The starfish

Lengthens and strengthens the back and buttock muscles. Like the dart, the movements are small but effective.

**The Exercise** 1. Lie on your front with your feet hip width apart, turned out from the hips. 2. Take your arms above your shoulders, elbows slightly bent, so that you look like a star. 3. Breathe in to prepare and lengthen through the spine. 4. Breathe out, zip up, and hollow. First lengthen then raise the opposite arm and leg an inch or two off the ground, lengthening away from the center. 5. Do not let the pelvis twist. Keep both hip joints on the floor. 6. Breathe in and relax. 7. Repeat five times each side.

**Take care** Your head and hip joints both stay on the floor. You should only lift your legs an inch or two.

aim to lift your legs an inch or two

do not overreach with the arms

keep both hip joints on the floor

keep pelvis square

# Child's pose

Another relaxation position to lengthen and stretch your back and inner thighs. Usually follows an exercise on your front.

**The Exercise** Come up on all fours with your feet together and your knees apart. Slowly move back toward your buttocks so you sit on your feet. Lower your chest to your thighs and your forehead to the floor. Rest and relax into this position.

**Take care** Do not strain the neck, stop if you feel uncomfortable in the lower back and avoid if you have knee problems.

back rounded

relax arms
and head

# The hundred

The first exercise of Joseph Pilates's original regime, the hundred can take months to perform in its original form. The exercise seriously tests the core muscles and their ability to support the upper body and legs while keeping the spine straight.

**The exercise** 1. Lie flat on your back with your arms by your sides, palms down. 2. Pull one knee toward your chest, and then pull in the other. The shin remains parallel to the floor. 3. Hover your hands a few inches off the mat, keeping them close to your body. 4. Lift your chin to your chest and begin pumping your arms up and down as if slapping water for five counts, resisting each pump so you feel it in your arms and belly. Do not touch the floor. 5. Exhale the air as you scoop your navel in and up.

**Take care** If your neck hurts, put it down, but keep pumping. The hundred is a challenge, not a pain.

shins parallel with floor

palms down

chin tucked in

# Roll up

Similar to a traditional "sit-up," the roll up strengthens your core muscles and keeps your spine flexible. It also increases the synovial fluids, the body's natural lubricant for your joints.

**The exercise** 1. Lie on your back with your knees together and bent, the soles of your feet firmly on the mat. Zip up and hollow. Wrap your hands behind the thighs and lift the elbows wide. 2. Inhale as you tighten your knees and buttocks and bring your chin to your chest, rolling upward and shaping your back into a C-curve. 3. Exhale as you straighten your legs and lean forward. Keep the chin down towards the chest. 4. Hold this position and take three deep breaths. 4. Lower down to the mat, one vertebra at a time. Repeat this sequence three times.

**Take care** Be careful if you have lower back pain.

elbows remain lifted

keep legs hip width apart

anchor feet to floor

spine in C-curve

# Leg circles

Leg circles strengthen the hips, create stability, and work the abdomen. Throughout the movement, anchor your body to the mat and use your leg like a paintbrush tracing circles in the air. Stabilize the pelvis and prevent the hips rocking from side to side.

**The Exercise** 1. Lie in the relaxation position, pressing your head and the back of your arms into the mat.
2. Raise your right leg up to the ceiling, slightly turning out from the hip. Control your pelvis so the hips do not shift. 3. Inhale to take the leg across the body. Sweep the leg down through the center line of your body and out in line with your right shoulder, tracing tiny circles in the air. Keep the upper leg as straight as possible. 4. Exhale and carry the leg back to the starting position. Circle five times, clockwise and counter-clockwise. Switch legs and repeat.

**Take care** Keep the pelvis still. Be careful if you have lower back pain or hip problems.

point your toe

trace tiny circles

do not crunch
back of neck

●●●

pin shoulder to the floor

# Rolling like a ball

Works the abdominals, improves balance, and improves spinal mobility.

**The Exercise** 1. Sit at the front of your mat with your knees bent in toward your chest, your knees open slightly. 2. Put your hands behind your knees and lift your feet off the mat so you balance on your tailbone. Your chin should be in, your elbows wide. 3. Zip up and hollow and begin to roll back. Do not throw your head back. Use your deep abdominals instead. 4. Inhale as you roll back. Exhale as you roll forward. 5. Repeat five or six times.

**Take care** Center your body to control your box and concentrate on precision and flow. Do not roll onto your neck or let your head touch the mat. Never let your feet open over the head. If stiff areas in the spine make it difficult to roll smoothly, place cushion under your back to assist roll.

feet should not go past head

elbows wide

head stays off the mat

keep eyes on abdominals

# Single leg stretch

Works your back muscles and stretches your back and legs.

**The Exercise** 1. Lie in the relaxation position. Breathe in.
2. Tuck your chin to your chest. Breathe out, zip up, and hollow
and fold one knee at a time up into your chest. 3. Breathe in, and
with both hands, take hold of your left leg. Keep your elbows open
and your breastbone soft. Your shoulder blades stay down into
your back and neck stays long. 4. Breathe out and extend
right leg, keeping left leg into chest. 5. Breathe in. 6. Breathe
out and come down. 6. Repeat ten times with each leg.

**Take Care** Your back must stay anchored to the floor.
If you experience any neck pain, rest it on a cushion.
Don't pull your knee to
your chest until your hip
is flexible.

straighten leg

tuck chin to
chest

keep tailbone down

firm buttocks

# Double leg stretch

This strengthens the abdominals, deep neck flexors, and leg muscles. Keep your head down if you have neck problems.

**The Exercise** 1. Lie with your knees bent towards your chest. Clasp your hands lightly behind your head. Keep your elbows open. 2. Breathe in to prepare. 3. Breathe out, scoop and hollow and slowly curl the head from the floor, keeping the neck soft and long and the chin gently tucked in. As you do so, straighten your legs but don't arch your back as you raise your legs. 4. The toes are softly pointed. 5. As you exhale, slowly lower your head to the floor, bending your knees onto your chest.

**Take care** Do not pull on the neck. Do not allow your legs to fall away from you. Keep your back anchored into the floor. Be careful if you have lower back problems.

toes softly pointed

keep upper body open

hands to support head

keep tailbone down

# Spine stretch forward

Stretches the spine and the hamstrings at the backs of the legs, as well as articulating the spine.

**The Exercise** 1. Sit tall with your legs extended on the mat, hip width apart. 2. Straighten your arms out at shoulder height. Keep your knees soft and flex your feet. 3. Breathe out and lower your head as though diving through your arms. Round forward with your upper back, leaving your lower back straight. 4. Zip up and hollow, stretching the lower back behind you. Aim the top of your head toward the mat. Do not lower the arms. 5. Breathe in to reverse the motion, curling up to a tall sitting position (as in step 1). Draw abdominals in to establish best posture.

**Take care**
Do not allow your back to flatten. Keep your legs aligned and be careful not to lean back.

head dives down

lower back stationary

arms reach out

toes point up

# Stretch and relax

Finish an exercise program with a full body stretch and relaxation. These work well as a final wind down but can also be used as instant relaxers at any time.

**The full body stretch** Lie down in relaxation position, your body in alignment and your pelvis in neutral. Extend your hands and fingers above your head and point your feet, keeping your toes relaxed. The more energy you put into the stretch the greater the sense of relaxation there will be when you release it.

**Relaxation** When you have finished the full body stretch, revert back to the relaxation position and stay like that for a few minutes. Breathe gently, letting any tension ebb away into the floor. Think kindly of yourself and your body, cultivating stillness and calm. After a few minutes, roll onto your side and then get up slowly. You will feel refreshed and alert, but with an inner tranquility that you can take into your every day life.

**Taking Pilates with you** Retraining your body can take a long time, but if you continue your practice regularly and use the wisdom of Pilates wherever you go then you will soon notice the difference: a stronger, leaner, and more confident you.

# glossary

**Alignment** The position or place where the joints of the body are both in line and symmetrical, particularly the spine and center.

**Articulate the spine** The movement of the spine that stacks your vertebra one at a time. A core concept used when peeling your spine up and down.

**Chin to chest** The safest position for your head, neck, and back; it works in line with gravity to hold your head in a safe position. The weight of the head is drawn toward the chest, without resulting tension.

**Contrology** The original name of Joseph Pilates's exercise method, now called "Pilates."

**Engagement** When you engage a muscle it is active and contracted during a movement. In Pilates you learn to engage muscles without bringing tension or stiffness into the action.

**Lateral breathing** Lateral breathing is a special way of breathing used in Pilates that expands the ribs sideways with each breath.

**Neutral pelvis** The position of the pelvis that creates the correct curves in the spine. If the top of the pelvis tips forward, the lumbar curve is exaggerated. If it tips back, the lumbar curve is flattened. In most Pilates exercises, the pelvis and spine need to be held in neutral.

**Pilates stance** In which feet are slightly turned out from the heels through a tensing of the gluteal or thigh muscles so that you make a small "V."

**Core muscles; powerhouse; girdle of strength** Band of muscles encircling the torso and extending from the lower ribcage to just below the buttocks.

**Spine to mat** Position in which you imagine your torso is anchored to the floor, giving you a firm base and preventing injury.

**Transverse abdominals** The transverse abdominal muscles wrap around the center of the body and provide support to the abdominal organs.

**Visualization** The act of creating images associated with the exercises such as "zipping up your abdomen."

**Wings down** The act of sliding or depressing the shoulder blades down the back and away from the neck and head. This helps to redress the effects of tension, which is often stored in this area.

**Zip up and hollow; navel to spine; scoop** The drawing inward and upward of the transverse adbominals, resulting in a hollow or scooped appearance in the waistline. This action engages the core muscles with the abdomen that support the spine and creates a strong and streamlined torso.

# further information

For further information and a directory of qualified pilates instructors in your area:
**Australia** www.pilates.net
**Canada** www.canadianpilatesassoc.com, www.stottconditioning.com
**USA** www.pilatesmethodalliance.org, www.pilates-studio.com

# index